Copyright © 2024 by Devin Henderson

All rights reserved.

Title: Buy Back Your Freedom: A Cargo Van Business Blueprint

Author: Devin Henderson Owner: Creative Faith Shipping LLC

No part of this publication may be reproduced, distributed, or transmitted in any form or by any means, including photocopying, recording, or other electronic or mechanical methods, without the prior written permission of the author or publisher, except in the case of brief quotations embodied in critical reviews and certain other noncommercial uses permitted by copyright law. For permission requests, please contact Creative Faith Shipping LLC at info@creativefaithplus.com.

This book is for informational purposes only. The author and publisher make no representations or warranties concerning the accuracy or completeness of the contents of this book and specifically disclaim any implied warranties of merchantability or fitness for a particular purpose. The advice and strategies contained herein may not be suitable for your situation. You should consult with a professional where appropriate. Neither the author nor the publisher shall be liable for any loss of profit or any other commercial damages, including but not limited to special, incidental, consequential, or other damages.
First Edition
ISBN-13: 979-8-3054-9485-3
Printed in the United States

Dedication Power Prayer in the bringing of this book:

The Lord Renews Our Mind DAILY.
In Jesus' Name We Pray. Amen. TYJ

Thank you, Jesus.

I want to give huge thanks to all my family: my wife Taylor, daughter Zaya, and son Zayden for being the "best" that a husband and father could ever imagine.

Illustrations Done by My Children

Disclaimer:

The websites and business names referenced in this book are included for informational purposes only and were accessed at the time of writing. The author does not endorse the content or accuracy of these websites, and readers are advised to verify information independently before making any decisions based on the material presented.

Table of Contents

Introduction	1
Chapter 1 Securing Contracts – The "Club 1000" Strategy	3
Chapter 2 Structuring Your Business	5
Chapter 3 Choosing The Right Cargo Van	7
Chapter 4 Fuel Up And Tool Up	9
Chapter 5 Building Client Relationships	11
Chapter 6 Managing Finances And Budgeting	13
Chapter 7 Scaling Your Business	15
Bonus Worksheet	18

INTRODUCTION

Freedom – What's the Cost?

Let's clear the windshield.

First things first: If you're looking for a quick get-rich scheme, this may not be the book for you.

However, if you're a truck driver like me, someone who doesn't come from a wealthy background (also me), or are seeking a low-overhead business opportunity, you're in the right place. Whether you're an adventurer who loves to travel and see the world or someone searching for a significant change in life, this is your road map.

You have the drive to potentially earn 2-3 times your current weekly salary. That's intriguing, isn't it?

This information I'm going to unpack took me countless hours of research and experience to gather, and I'm honored to give you access to it, saving you thousands of dollars and countless mistakes.

This is your chance to power your freedom back and start a legacy.

Hello, I'm Devin Henderson. I own CreativeFaithPlus and have over five years of experience in the logistics field.

Congratulations on taking the wheel toward your successful cargo van courier business. Jump in the passenger seat and ride with me through these simple steps. With precision, faith, and hard work, you're destined for success.

Let's Go

CHAPTER 1

Securing Contracts – The "Club 1000" Strategy

Stop laughing! I'm serious. The foundation of any cargo van courier business is securing consistent work. Without this, scaling your business becomes impossible.

Choosing Your Service Type

Decide what type of service you'll provide:

- Long-Haul: Travel across 48 multiple states.
- Regional: Staying closer to home could be your "Bread and Butter."
- Local/Dedicated Routes: Returning home safely every night.

Where to Find Work

Searching your local community is a good start and easier than ever with the help of modern-day technology on the internet. Start there by using major platforms like Google and Chat GPT, which makes it a literal breeze. From Gig apps and contracts to medical courier opportunities, your wheels should stay rolling.

Here are platforms to explore opportunities:

- Gig Apps: Dlivrd.io, Dispatch.com, GoShare.com
- Medical Courier Work: MedZoomer.com, Labexp.com, Dropoff.com.

- Freight Services: DAT.com, OneRail.com, Curri Driver.com
- General Contracts: CBDriver.com, Indeed.com, Craigslist.com

These resources open endless doors for your business. Take advantage of them and keep your wheels turning.

Chapter 2

Structuring Your Business

Creating the right foundation for your business is key to long-term success. This includes choosing the right business structure and developing a unique brand.

Naming and Branding

Exploring your multiple colorways of business structure whether it's a side hustle or creating your own LLC (limited liability company). Structuring your business takes strategic planning and execution. Think creatively for a name and logo that stands out. Tools like ChatGPT or LegalZoom's business name generator can help with the heavy lifting. For a professional logo, explore AI-powered platforms like Canva or Tailor Brands.

Choosing a Legal Structure

Options include:

- LegalZoom
- Zen-business
- Tailor Brands
- Fiver

Platforms like LegalZoom and Zen-Business exclusively make setting up your entity seamless. Don't forget to consult a licensed CPA or attorney to guide you through tax and legal compliance.

Setting Up a Business Bank Account

Prepare for success by separating your personal and business finances, you'll thank yourself later for the organization. Many banks offer accounts tailored for small businesses.

Popular Bank Options:

- Novo.co
- Navyfederal.org
- Bankofamerica.com

Chapter
3
Choosing the Right Cargo Van

> We all know it's important to sport the proper footwear on our feet for the occasion. Likewise finding the proper cargo-van or sprinter van goes as such.

These are a few selections from the leading class of vehicles for such work.

- Ford Transit Series
- Ram Pro-Master Series
- Nissan NV Series

They come in multiple sizes, engine types to different colors as well. If you happen to purchase a used van (Which I prefer for starters) be sure to have a thorough inspection done! I would even go as far as purchasing an extended warranty. Your van is your office, and choosing the right one is crucial.

Insurance

You need to get quoted. Research insurance policies based on your service type. Now this is a daunting task to fulfill but trust me we will- for sure fit underneath that low clearance bridge with ease. Larger contracts often require $1 million-dollar premium coverage, with included cargo. Be sure to check with the company's contract on behalf of exactly what you need.

You have many different insurance companies out there like...

- Progressive
- GEICO
- Liberty Mutual

In some cases, you can find the vehicle's VIN number online while browsing in the specs section. This could be helpful if you want to get quoted before you purchase a van.

Chapter 4

Fuel Up and Tool Up

Taking care of your van is essential for minimizing downtime and maximizing profits. Regular maintenance keeps you rolling smoothly. By factoring in Preventative maintenance (PM) save yourself the frustration of breakdowns.

This is a basic checklist to take to your mechanic or if you hold a "crafty tool belt" you can do it on your own.

Maintenance Checklist

- Oil changes and tire rotations: Every 3,000 miles.
- Transmission flush: Every 60,000 miles.
- Coolant and brake system checks.
- Spark plug replacement.

Keep $5,000 in a maintenance reserve account for unexpected repairs. If you do not have $5,000, do not worry. As you secure work you can easily start properly planning these funds into your maintenance bucket.

Fuel Savings

Believe it or not- FUEL is your biggest expense. There's no way around it, trust me—I've tried.

Unless you roll electric.

With rising fuel prices, it is crucial to actively seek deals. Use these resources down below to tap into some savings.

- Loves.com

- Gasbuddy.com
- Mudflapinc.com

Chapter 5

Building Client Relationships

Back to the basics - Communication is Key

On-Time Delivery, Every Time

Your business thrives on repeat customers and strong relationships. To achieve long-term success, it's essential to cultivate professionalism and responsiveness in all your interactions. Always communicate effectively with every party you're contracted with, ensuring that expectations are clear and met with precision. Regularly update your clients on delivery statuses and address any issues promptly and courteously. This not only demonstrates reliability but also builds trust and strengthens your reputation in the industry.

Reputation and Opportunity

Mastering time management and reliability can significantly boost your reputation. A strong reputation not only ensures client retention but also attracts new clients through word-of-mouth referrals and positive online reviews. Always remember that your reputation is your most asset in this line of work.

Contractual Obligations

Carefully review your contracts before signing to understand the expectations and requirements fully. Most agreements will emphasize timeliness and dependability as (non-negotiable terms). Failing to adhere to these terms can lead to financial penalties and even potential termination of your contract.

Therefore, it is vital to prioritize punctuality and reliability to avoid unnecessary setbacks.

The Value of Direct Shippers

Direct shippers are invaluable in this business. Unlike other arrangements, working with direct shippers often comes with more flexible delivery schedules. This flexibility can make your work more manageable and rewarding. Strive to establish and nurture these connections, as they represent golden opportunities within this industry.

Strong relationships, reliable performance, and a commitment to excellence will ensure your business not only survives but thrives in a competitive marketplace.

Chapter 6

Managing Finances and Budgeting

The Key to Long-Term Business Success:
Smart Financial Management

Managing your money effectively is the backbone of a thriving cargo van business! With the right tools and strategies, you can take control of your finances, reduce stress, and set your business up for success.

Let's break it down:

Keep Tabs on Your Expenses

Think of tracking expenses as giving yourself a clear picture of where your money is going and quickly spot opportunities to save money and make smarter spending choices.

This isn't as hard as it sounds—there are amazing apps like QuickBooks, Wave, and Genius Scan to help you out.

Here's how to make it work for you:

- Monitor income and spending. Stay aware of every dollar coming in and going out.

- Categorize expenses by grouping your spending (e.g., fuel, repairs, insurance) this will help you in the long run.
- Save those receipts! Use cloud storage to keep digital copies of all business-related receipts. It's safer and way easier to organize than a stack of papers!

Don't worry—compared to other industries, these costs are manageable. With the right mindset and planning, you can handle budgeting with ease!

You Got This!

Managing your business finances might feel overwhelming at first, but with a little practice and the right tools, it becomes second nature. You're building something amazing, and every step you take toward better financial management is a step toward long-term success. Stay confident, stay organized, and remember:

> You're in control of your business's future!

Chapter 7

Scaling Your Business

SPRINTERS, on your Mark, Set, GO

Scaling Your Cargo Van Courier Business

Congratulations! You've laid the foundation for your courier business. Now, it's time to think bigger and take your operations to the next level. Growth is exciting and rewarding, but it takes strategy and smart decisions. Let's break it down:

Expand Your Fleet

As demand for your services grows, so should your fleet! Adding more vans and progressively box trucks allows you to take on bigger jobs and serve more clients. Here's how to approach it:

- Start smart by adding vehicles one at a time as your business grows. This keeps costs manageable and ensures you can handle the additional workload.
- Diversify your fleet. Different types of vehicles can handle different kinds of deliveries. A smaller van might be great for city routes, while larger vehicles can take care of bulk or long-haul jobs.
- Keep efficiency in mind. Choose vehicles that are cost-effective and fuel-efficient to maximize your profits.

By expanding strategically, you'll be ready to handle any delivery needs that come your way!

Hire and Train Reliable Drivers

You can't do everything on your own, and that's okay! Adding drivers to your team is a big step, but it's also an important one for scaling your business.

- Find the right people. Look for dependable individuals who value professionalism and customer service as much as you do.
- Invest in training. Teach your drivers the ins and outs of the job—whether it's efficient delivery routes, safety tips, or how to represent your business with pride.
- Build a strong team culture. Treat your drivers well, and they'll be more likely to stay and help your business succeed.

With a skilled and reliable team in place, you'll have the manpower to take on more jobs and grow your reputation as a top-notch courier service.

Build a Solid Network

No business grows in isolation. Expanding your connections can help you open new doors and attract more opportunities.

- Partner with other courier businesses. Collaborating with others allows you to exchange leads, fill in gaps during busy times, and tackle larger jobs together.
- Join industry groups and associations like the CLDA. Networking with other professionals in the logistics field can help you learn best practices, gain referrals, and build your credibility.
- Keep communication open. Stay in touch with your partners and clients—they're the backbone of your business growth.

By building a strong network, you'll broaden your reach and become part of a supportive community that helps each other thrive.

Your Business, Your Future

Scaling your cargo van courier business is a journey, but every step you take brings you closer to greater success. Keep your vision clear, your strategy solid, and your energy high. With smart decisions and a willingness to grow, the sky's the limit for what you can achieve seriously.

> You've got the drive—now it's time to take your business to the next level!

BONUS WORKSHEET

Used to help you outline short-term and long-term business goals.

> Now that you have the roadmap to freedom, it's time to execute. Success doesn't happen overnight, but with persistence, faith, and a solid strategy, you'll reach your goals.

Need more guidance? My email is listed at the end of this book. I offer one-on-one coaching to help you get your business up and running in no time.

Thank you all for taking the time to endeavor towards a significant leap of faith in creating a legacy of your own in the Logistics Industry.

Blessings be to everyone,

STAY TUNED FOR PART 2:

- Starting Your Own Authority
- Marketing Your Business
- Hiring Drivers
- Investing Your Revenue

Devin Henderson
Owner
Creative Faith Shipping LLC
info@creativefaithplus.com

www.ingramcontent.com/pod-product-compliance
Lightning Source LLC
Chambersburg PA
CBHW071000220526
45471CB00007B/3107